ECONOMIC ISSUES 14



# Lessons from Systemic Bank Restructuring

Claudia Dziobek
Ceyla Pazarbaşıoğlu

INTERNATIONAL MONETARY FUND
WASHINGTON, D.C.

Cover design and composition:
Massoud Etemadi, Julio Prego, and
the IMF Graphics Section

ISBN 1-55775-739-9
ISSN 1020-5098

Published April 1998

Reprinted November 1998

To order IMF publications, please contact:

International Monetary Fund, Publication Services
700 19th Street, N.W., Washington, D.C. 20431, U.S.A.
Tel: (202) 623-7430 Telefax: (202) 623-7201
E-mail: publications@imf.org
Internet: http://www.imf.org

## Preface

The Economic Issues series aims to make available to a broad readership of nonspecialists some of the economic research being produced on topical issues by the staff of the IMF. The raw material of the series is drawn mainly from IMF Working Papers, technical papers produced by IMF staff members and visiting scholars, as well as from policy-related research papers.

This Economic Issue draws on material originally contained in IMF Working Paper 97/161, "Lessons from Systemic Bank Restructuring: A Survey of 24 Countries," by Claudia Dziobek and Ceyla Pazarbaşıoğlu. It also draws on a chapter by the same authors, "Lessons and Elements of Best Practice," from an IMF book, *Systemic Bank Restructuring and Macroeconomic Policy,* edited by William E. Alexander, Jeffrey M. Davis, Liam P. Ebrill, and Carl-Johan Lindgren. The current version was partially redrafted and edited by Charles S. Gardner. Readers may purchase the book ($23.50) and the Working Paper ($7.00) from IMF Publication Services, or view the latter in full text on the IMF's website (http://www.imf.org).

# Lessons from Systemic Bank Restructuring

In recent decades, many countries have experienced banking problems requiring a major—and expensive—overhaul of their banking systems. Often, the problems have domestic causes, such as weak banking supervision, political interference, and inadequate capital. Or a country's banking system may be outmoded and in need of rebuilding, as in the case of many developing countries and all countries moving from centrally planned to market economies. Outside forces, such as a fall in the price of a key export product or commodity, can ignite or worsen a crisis.

Ideally the national authorities should anticipate the need for reforms and carry them out in times of relative financial calm. Too often, however, a banking crisis occurs before countries can muster the political will to undertake essential reforms. In a banking crisis, depositors, lenders to banks, and owners of bank capital all lose confidence and seek simultaneously to salvage their resources by withdrawing them. A single bank can fail without national repercussions, but when a large proportion of the deposits in a national banking system are involved, the problem becomes systemic and paralysis threatens the economy. The government has no option but to act, and the remedies available in crisis are more difficult and costly.

Countries take many different approaches to resolving their banking crises, with differing degrees of success. Useful lessons can be learned by examining country experiences and comparing the approaches taken with the results achieved. The lessons emerge clearly when countries are ranked by the success of their reform efforts and by comparing their use of the available strategies, policies, and tools for reform.

For this purpose, the authors of the study analyzed the experiences of 24 countries that initiated reforms in the 1980s and early 1990s: 4 industrial and 15 developing countries, and 5 countries in transition to market-oriented systems. They considered a banking crisis systemic if a fifth or more of the total deposits in the national system was affected. All areas of the world were represented.

This Economic Issue explains which practices lead to successful restructuring. It then relates illustrative cases of several countries' restructurings.

But first, what is meant by "systemic bank restructuring"?

## Defining Systemic Bank Restructuring

Systemic bank restructuring aims to improve bank performance—that is, restore solvency and profitability, improve the banking system's capacity to provide financial intermediation between savers and borrowers, and restore public confidence.

Roughly speaking, *financial restructuring* tries to restore *solvency* (net worth) by improving banks' balance sheets. A bank can improve its balance sheet by raising additional capital (e.g., receiving cash from existing or new owners or from the government), by reducing liabilities (e.g., writing down the value of certain debts), or by boosting the value of assets (e.g., raising the recovery value of problem loans and collateral). *Operational restructuring* affects *profitability*. Measures can include renewed attention to business strategy, improved management and accounting systems, and better credit assessment and approval techniques. Operating costs may be cut by eliminating branches and staff.

To add to the banking system's capacity for intermediation, restructuring usually means improving supervision and prudential regulation. Sometimes other measures, such as providing deposit insurance and a lender of last resort, are also needed.

## The Country Cases

The country experiences were ranked by relative progress in resolving banking sector problems, that is, banking performance and changes in financial system intermediation capacity. Two aspects of bank performance were considered: solvency and sustainable profitability. Indicators used to assess bank solvency included the ratio of nonperforming loans to total loans and the ratio of capital to assets. Indicators used to assess bank profitability included the ratio of operating expenses to assets, the ratio of interest income to assets, and the ratio of profits to assets. The authors used six indicators to measure the improvement in the financial intermediation capacity of the banking system: the ratio of the growth of credit to the private sector to GDP growth; the ratio of broad money to GDP; changes in interest spreads; central bank credit to banks as a percentage of GDP; changes in the real interest rate; and experiences with recurrent banking problems.

Based on these indicators of improvement, we grouped countries into three broad categories: those that made substantial progress in

**Table 1. Results and Costs of Banking Reforms**

*(Reforms begun in year shown; costs are cumulative fiscal outlays in percent of GDP, not including government cost recoveries)*

| Substantial Progress | Cost | Moderate Progress | Cost | Slow Progress | Cost |
|---|---|---|---|---|---|
| Côte d'Ivoire (1991) | 13.0 | Chile (1983) | 33.0 | Kuwait (1992) | 45.0 |
| Peru (1991) | 0.4 | Egypt (1991) | . . . | Mauritania (1993) | 15.0 |
| Philippines (1984) | 4.0 | Finland (1991) | 9.9 | Tanzania (1992) | 14.0 |
| Spain (1980) | 15.0 | Ghana (1989) | 6.0 | | |
| Sweden (1991) | 4.3 | Hungary (1993) | 12.2 | | |
| | | Korea (1993) | . . . | | |
| | | Poland (1993) | 5.7 | | |

restructuring their banking systems, those that made moderate progress, and those that made slow progress (see Table 1). Nine countries (Argentina, Indonesia, Japan, Kazakhstan, Latvia, Mexico, Moldova, Venezuela, and Zambia) that started their reforms later (after 1994) were studied but were excluded from the ranking because the results of their efforts could not be clearly assessed.

**Table 2. Use and Effectiveness of Restructuring Tools**

*(Percent of countries in each group)*

| | Substantial Progress (5) | Moderate Progress (7) | Slow Progress (3) | Recent Reforms (9) |
|---|---|---|---|---|
| **Structural measures** | | | | |
| Central bank as sole restructuring agency | 20 | 57 | 100 | 89 |
| Central bank liquidity support | 40 | 86 | 100 | 100 |
| Loan workout units (public- or bank-based) | 100 | 86 | 67 | 56 |
| Closure of insolvent banks | 80 | 57 | 33 | 67 |
| Merger of insolvent banks | 60 | 86 | 33 | 44 |
| Privatization (where applicable) | 100 | 100 | 33 | 71 |
| Enterprise restructuring to improve creditors | 40 | 71 | 0 | 44 |
| Twinning with foreign banks | 20 | 29 | 0 | 22 |
| **Financial measures** | | | | |
| Bonds (e.g., exchanged for bad loans) | 100 | 86 | 100 | 56 |
| New equity (e.g., bought by government) | 60 | 57 | 33 | 44 |
| Depositor-based instruments | 60 | 57 | 67 | 44 |
| Owner, management market incentives | 100 | 71 | 33 | 78 |
| *Average number of instruments used* | *8* | *9* | *7* | *8* |

The authors then related the rankings to the particular policy tools used by countries in their restructuring operations and examined the accompanying economic conditions and policies. Table 2 shows the effectiveness of some of the main instruments used for bank restructuring.

## Best Practices

The lessons take the form of a set of "best practices." Guiding principles such as these must always be considered in the light of specific circumstances, since individual country situations will always differ. Nevertheless, a clear understanding of what has worked or failed in the past is important in guiding countries that are formulating their own plans for reforms. This is particularly true since the plans so often are forged under crisis conditions—including runs on banks and capital flight—when speed is essential.

Indeed, prompt corrective action is a key ingredient of successful banking reform. The countries making substantial progress all took action within a year of the emergence of their banking problems. They also effectively diagnosed the nature and extent of the problems, identified the underlying causes, and designed a restructuring strategy to address them all systematically. In all 24 countries, systemic problems had multiple causes, and chances for success were greatest when the causes were diagnosed accurately, then addressed swiftly and comprehensively.

In general, countries making slow progress faced more problems. They had particular difficulties correcting taxation policies that distorted incentives in banking and, where state-owned banks had problems, countries often refused, or failed, to confront them. In the countries that made good progress, sudden outside events, like the collapse of export prices or soaring world interest rates, often triggered the banking crises, forcing the countries to undertake comprehensive reform.

### *Solvency: Just the First Step*

Successful reform invariably requires resisting a tendency to be satisfied when solvency is restored, allowing troubled banks to resume lending. Experience shows that these banks are soon likely to be in trouble again unless conditions are also established for restoring their profitability. This means following through with needed changes in management and cutting operating costs. It also requires strengthening the accounting, legal, and regulatory systems, and backing up these reforms with firm, consistent supervision and compliance.

These operational reforms are necessary for banks to return to sustained solvency and profitability. All countries making substantial progress, and most with moderate success, emphasized operational restructuring. By contrast, of the three slow-progress countries, while two addressed regulatory and accounting issues, only one dealt with poor management. Management deficiencies caused problems in all 24 countries, and successful reform depended directly on correcting them.

Countries are far more successful in restoring solvency than they are in promoting gains in profitability. Governments find it quick and relatively easy to make progress against insolvency, through such means as swapping bonds for nonperforming loans, and they often overemphasize such remedies. Achieving profitability requires painful operational restructuring, which is more difficult and time-consuming.

### *Who Takes the Lead?*

A tricky aspect of successful reform strategies involves defining the right role for the central bank—to be supportive but not involved operationally. When the central bank is the lead agency, it often gets drawn into financing bank restructuring measures, exceeding its resources, and taking actions that conflict with its basic responsibilities for monetary management. A far better approach is to designate a separate lead agency to coordinate and implement the restructuring. To be effective, the lead agency must be equipped to undertake steady, focused monitoring of restructuring policies, as well as individual bank restructuring operations if necessary. Monitoring is vital because bank restructuring requires a number of years and usually involves large public expenditures.

The countries surveyed that made only slow progress all relied excessively on the central bank, using it as lead agency for restructuring, as well as for both immediate liquidity support and medium-term financing. The moderate-progress countries relied significantly less on their central banks, while those making substantial progress used the central bank as lead agency in only a fifth of the cases; less than half of these countries used the central bank for liquidity support, and just over half for medium-term financing. Countries that achieved the best results determined at an early stage that the problems were bank insolvencies, not merely a lack of liquidity, and this precluded the extensive use of central bank lender of last resort facilities.

Even if a separate lead agency is designated, the central bank must stand ready to provide liquidity support during restructuring to viable banks. Many countries used temporary or permanent reduction of reserve requirements, broad application of discounting facilities, or short-term loans to provide liquidity. Certainly, best practice is to minimize reliance on protracted liquidity support. Nor should the central bank provide long-term financing to banks, or engage in commercial banking activities, as these exceed its financial resources. Essential long-term outlays should be made through direct, clearly identifiable government expenditures or they will create conflicts with the central bank's monetary policy responsibilities.

Few countries surveyed refrained from using short-term liquidity support; but the most successful countries minimized the use of central bank financing and avoided central bank lending to insolvent banks. Nevertheless, government financial support of illiquid banks was unavoidable in most instances. Bond transfers and other financial instruments were widely used for this purpose, but not always successfully.

### Sharing the Loss

The principle of loss sharing among the state, the banks, and the public is integral to successful bank restructuring. One way to incorporate loss-sharing arrangements into the overall strategy is through a deposit insurance entity funded by contributions from banks. Although the authorities avoided imposing outright losses on depositors in most countries, Côte d'Ivoire, Latvia, Peru, and Spain have successfully imposed limited losses on depositors and other creditors without causing a panic or a run on banks.

Removing nonperforming loans from the banks' balance sheets and transferring them to a separate loan recovery agency can be an effective way of addressing the banks' solvency problems. The authors' research shows that most substantial-progress and moderate-progress countries did this. Carving out nonperforming loans immediately improved the banks' balance sheets and freed them to focus attention on their core business. This did not, however, solve the banks' problems of low profitability.

Loan workout (foreclosure or asset sales) is important to recover some of the cost of bank restructuring and to send signals to delinquent borrowers. Loan workouts can be done by a central organization, usually operated by the state, or by special loan collection agencies tied to individual banks, an approach Sweden used successfully in 1991. The survey results suggest that the institutional setting does not matter. Some countries, including Chile, the Philippines, and the transition countries, approached the loan workout issue indirectly by providing debt relief to borrowers by engaging simultaneously in the restructuring of borrowing enterprises themselves.

Finally, successful restructuring requires clear policies for determining when a bank is viable or when it should simply be permitted to fail. Countries with successful reform efforts established clear standards and applied them consistently.

## *Issues in State Ownership*

State-owned banks pose special problems. Privatization or closure of these banks worked well in many countries, but the design of privatization is very important in determining banks' future profitability and viability. Experiences in Chile and Mexico demonstrate that a rapid and ill-designed process of bank privatization can contain the seeds of subsequent banking crises. In both cases, preferential access to credit given to some bidders, overpricing of bank assets, and weak legislation against concentration of ownership allowed a few large business conglomerates to acquire a large portion of the financial system. In both cases, the government later had to take over all of these banks, either for insolvency or for lending excessively to affiliated companies.

Special problems exist, too, in the former centrally planned economies. When the countries of the former Soviet Union began to embark on market-oriented reforms in 1991–92, two-tier banking systems emerged with the creation of central banks and the transformation of specialized state banks into notionally independent commercial banks. Many of the latter institutions, lacking experience in credit evaluation, engaged in aggressive lending to enterprises to which they had ownership or other ties. At first, the consequences of poor credit evaluation were masked by high inflation. But then successful stabilization programs began to cut inflation sharply, revealing the banks' underlying weaknesses and touching off a panic. Banking crisis can also be sparked—as in Latvia—when the government moves to impose stronger prudential standards, and the extent of bank weaknesses is exposed to the public.

Clearly, bank restructuring in these countries is an arduous and time-consuming task that, in most cases, is only just beginning. Governments must build practically the entire operating framework of the banking system, including the courts and legal system. With basic banking skills in critically short supply, the central bank is often the only institution available to build the financial system required to support market-based commercial banking activity. In the meantime, the fragility of the banking system severely constrains the economic recovery of most transitional economies.

## *The Economic Environment*

Experience holds few clues to the direct relationship between bank restructuring efforts and economic conditions. While an environment of strong economic growth helps bank restructuring operations, the study's empirical results give examples where measures have succeeded even where the economic situation remained weak. This is consistent with the principle that prompt government action is required to take difficult and unpalatable measures, without waiting for a serendipitous upturn in the economy.

In all the experiences studied, the trend of inflation was the most consistent development; it declined in nearly all countries in the years after bank restructuring began. One possible reason is that countries recognized that inflating their way out of banking system problems was no answer. Another is that the losses of wealth associated with banking crises often sharply reduced domestic demand. Whatever the cause, restructuring is likely to take place in an environment of disinflation. This should minimize concerns about the inflationary effects of short-term liquidity injections by the central bank to support banking reforms, or about tightening monetary conditions during restructuring. At the same time, the budget often deteriorates immediately following the onset of bank restructuring, in part because the costs of economic restructuring are so high.

Although bank restructuring programs may be initiated in a time of economic stagnation or severe recession, positive economic growth helps banks to resume lending and return to profitability.

## Country Experiences

### *Côte d'Ivoire: Success Through Comprehensiveness*

Côte d'Ivoire's successful restructuring, which began in 1991, shows the importance of a comprehensive approach. As early as 1986, deteriorating world market prices of cocoa and coffee began to take their toll on the country's fragile banking system, and over the next two years, liquidation was started for four of the five state development banks. By 1990, the 14 commercial banks were experiencing a sharp drop in deposits and credits from foreign banks.

In 1991, the government started a comprehensive restructuring plan with World Bank support. Quickly, the last state bank was placed in liquidation, new laws were enacted to provide for the foreclosure and management of nonperforming loans, and the commercial banks were recapitalized through the settlement of government arrears and new capital from private owners. In an important signal of government seriousness, owners of insolvent commercial banks were given the choice of closing and liquidating, or injecting fresh capital, with none considered too big to fail. The recapitalization, backed up by the regional central bank, the Central Bank of West African States (BCEAO), restored liquidity, and commercial banks were able to resume lending on a small scale by 1992.

A package of operational reforms bolstered the successful restoration of liquidity. These included management changes and cuts in the staffs and branches of the commercial banks. The government strengthened the framework of regulatory, accounting, fiscal, legal, and monetary policies. For example, legal reforms empowered the banks to collect on collateral and foreclose on delinquent borrowers. And in mid-1991, the authorities introduced new prudential provisions, including stronger capital adequacy requirements and lending limits to single borrowers. A newly formed regional Banking Commission provided continuing supervision, including regular bank audits.

Completed in 1992, these reforms provided the groundwork for improved bank performance. By 1994, the banks' return on capital rose to almost 10 percent, and most banks had returned to compliance with the newly toughened prudential rules. At first, the country's economic recovery remained weak, but it improved from the start of 1994, following the devaluation of the CFA franc and the introduction of other macroeconomic and structural changes supported by the IMF. This renewed growth was an important underlying condition for restoring the soundness of Côte d'Ivoire's banking system.

### *Mauritania: Need for Comprehensiveness*

Just as in Côte d'Ivoire, weak world markets for two of Mauritania's important industries, agriculture and fishing, put severe pressure in 1988–89 on the country's poorly managed banking system. With World Bank help, the government undertook a restructuring program in 1988–90 to sell the country's industrial development bank and the state's majority ownership of its four commercial banks to the private sector.

To pave the way, the government built up the banks' balance sheets by absorbing their large overdrafts with the central bank. Lack of political consensus undermined a planned program of operational reforms, however, and they received little attention. The banks continued to lend to the troubled agricultural and fishing industries, and made little effort to improve the quality of their portfolios. The central bank proved unable to exercise effective supervision, including compliance with its prudential requirements. Privatization plans lagged, and recovery of nonperforming loans bogged down in long, costly legal procedures. By the end of 1991, the banks' nonperforming loans reached 50 percent of their credit to the private sector, and it was apparent that the restructuring had not succeeded.

In 1992–94, the government made use of the IMF's concessional facility to assist low-income countries—the Enhanced Structural Adjustment Facility—to support a second effort at restructuring. The development bank was closed and its assets liquidated, the four commercial banks were recapitalized and fully privatized, and the central bank's supervisory powers were strengthened. The government established a loan recovery agency and achieved its target for

1995. Overall, the cost to the government of the second restructuring effort was about 7.6 percent of GDP, with more than half used to liquidate the development bank. Mauritania's banks showed signs of increased profitability in 1995, and its overall experience illustrated that banking problems will surely recur if financial restructuring is not accompanied by operational reforms.

### Sweden: Fast Action Is Key

Sweden weathered a severe banking crisis in the early 1990s with a comprehensive restructuring strategy, and did so while minimizing the cost of its restructuring program. Formation of a broad political consensus distinguished the effort, as the government provided Parliament with extensive information to foster bipartisan support and invited the opposition to all main meetings. Transparency and disclosure of information were crucial for regaining confidence domestically and abroad.

The crisis started in late 1990, when recession and overlending to the real estate industry led to a surge of loan losses for Swedish banks. The government stepped in with capital injections and loan guarantees. In December 1992, the Parliament guaranteed that bank obligations would be met and set up a new Bank Support Authority (BSA) as the lead restructuring agency. Firm standards were set to determine which banks could and could not be saved, the BSA was charged with approving all bank requests for guarantees, and most banks set up workout subsidiaries to deal with their nonperforming loans, freeing bank management to deal with core business.

Unlike a number of countries, where government bonds were exchanged for nonperforming bank loans, Sweden paid the cost of the guarantees and the capital injections from the budget as needed. At its peak, the government's total commitment was 5.9 percent of GDP. Most of the cost was in capital injections, and only a few banks actually used the government assistance. Ultimately, the cost to the budget amounted to 4.2 percent of GDP, and that is declining over time through loan recoveries and sales of appreciated shares of Nordbanken, the now-profitable state-owned bank, which is being privatized. With no applications for support received in 1994–96, the guarantee program was phased out.

### Chile and Spain: Role of the Central Bank

In the early 1980s, both Spain and Chile suffered systemic bank problems. Spain's problems began to surface first, triggered by the aftereffects of the oil price increases of the 1970s. In Chile, severe recession was worsened by the rise of U.S. interest rates to historic levels. Copper prices plunged, capital fled the country, the peso fell 90 percent against the U.S. dollar, and arrears built rapidly on the foreign-exchange-linked loans outstanding to domestic borrowers.

In the years leading up to these problems, the banking systems in both countries liberalized, expanded, and took increasing risks with inadequate legal, regulatory, and accounting systems for proper risk management. Both countries embarked on comprehensive bank restructuring, Spain in 1980 and Chile in 1983. In both, the central bank took the lead in devising, carrying out, and financing the strategy. In Chile, the central bank took over 14 of 26 commercial banks and 8 of 17 private domestic finance companies. It ultimately liquidated eight of the banks and all of the finance companies, becoming directly involved in the lending operations of the banks.

Both countries ultimately restored bank soundness and strengthened bank supervision, but Spain achieved success more rapidly and at lower cost. There, banking sector soundness was largely restored by the mid-1980s at a cumulative cost of about 15 percent of output. The cost in Chile ultimately amounted to about a third of a year's output, and four years into its restructuring, bank capital ratios were still below their pre-crisis levels, bank profitability remained low, and operating expenses were too high.

Why the differences? In Spain, the central bank emphasized cost sharing with the banking community and put in place other incentives for improved corporate governance. Moreover, the Bank of Spain removed its bank activities from its monetary policy and supervisory duties and placed them in a separate Deposit Guarantee Fund (FGD). The Central Bank of Chile, in contrast, undertook continuing fiscal expenditures by assuming the financial costs of bank rescue operations. Cost sharing in Chile deferred the burden on bank owners to the future, and in the end the Central Bank of Chile absorbed much of it. In addition, the Central Bank of Chile became actively engaged in debt rescheduling and in commercial bank lending, and in effect continued the operations of insolvent banks.

In Spain, rehabilitation followed a sequence the authorities dubbed "accordion" recapitalization. First, existing bad debts were written off against remaining capital. Then, the FGD acquired a controlling interest in the bank, and later injected cash for additional equity stakes, finally selling the bank to new shareholders. Since the old owners lost their equity, incentives were strong for improved corporate management.

### *The Philippines: Rehabilitating State Banks*

The Philippines' reform effort that began in 1984 highlights the special problems of dealing with state-owned banks. It is also a good example of a sudden unfavorable turn in the global economic environment exposing severe weaknesses in the banking system and triggering a successful banking reform.

In the late 1970s, the rise in international interest rates made it increasingly difficult for the Philippines to service its external debt, and the government declared a moratorium in 1983 that led to financial panic, a run on banks, and capital flight. Although these developments increased financial fragility, the root of the Philippines' banking crisis lay within the financial sector.

Weaknesses in regulation and lax banking practices magnified the crisis. In its effort to prop up the economy, the government directed banks to lend to enterprises in distress, and the supervisory agency (the Monetary Board) waived enforcement of banking standards to give troubled banks a chance to overcome financial difficulties. By the end of 1985, the two largest state-owned banks, with about half of the banking system's assets—the Philippines National Bank (PNB) and the Development Bank of the Philippines (DPB)—were insolvent. A comprehensive rehabilitation program began with getting nonperforming loans off the two banks' balance sheets and covering them with government debt, which was paid off over three years. A new agency, the Assets Privatization Trust, was set up to conduct loan workouts and recovery operations.

The Philippines' success included proper diagnosis of the problem, operational reforms to back up the financial restructuring, and strengthened regulation and prudential standards. Measures to rehabilitate the state-owned banks, which accounted for most of the problems, concentrated on substantial operational restructuring, including new management and major cost reduction. All tax privileges were withdrawn from the banks, public deposits were limited to working balances, the banks were subjected to private external audits, and the government withdrew all further guarantees. With the profitability of the banks restored, the way was paved for successful privatization. The Philippines' successful banking reform increased its resistance to the Asian financial crisis that broke out in 1997.

## The Lessons

The study found that the resumption of bank lending and a return to profitability requires prompt corrective action and a comprehensive approach. Policymakers must address the immediate problems of weak and insolvent banks, shortcomings in accounting, legal, and regulatory frameworks, and lax supervision and compliance. During the restructuring, the central bank must also stand ready to provide liquidity support to viable banks. The central bank should not, however, provide long-term financing to banks, nor should it be involved in commercial banking activities, as this leads to substantial fiscal costs and creates conflicts with its monetary policy objectives.

Failing to manage the nonperforming assets of all banks, as well as the remaining assets of failed banks, raises the total cost of restructuring. It also creates an inequitable distribution of losses by rewarding defaulters and by impairing incentives for debt repayment in the future. Loan workout units, decentralized or centralized, that are actively managed to maximize returns and maintain asset values can contribute to the recovery of bank restructuring costs and send the appropriate signals to delinquent borrowers.

In instances where difficulties were concentrated in state-owned banks, the problem banks were sometimes privatized. The design of privatization is important. In some cases, preferences were given to bidders that did not have the necessary banking skills; in other cases, bank assets were poorly priced. Country experiences show that poorly designed programs contain the seeds of subsequent banking crises.

All countries included in the study were much more successful in addressing *solvency* problems than *profitability* problems. One explanation is that improvement in bank solvency emanates chiefly from shorter-term financial restructuring, while a return to profitability requires more difficult, longer-term operational restructuring. Swapping bonds for nonperforming loans, for example, instantly improves solvency indicators, but does not necessarily affect costs, earnings, or profits. And, in practice, the design of bank restructuring packages is often somewhat unbalanced, focusing more on financial restructuring measures at the expense of operational restructuring measures.

As to improvements in financial intermediation, results indicate substantial variation across country groups: while countries usually were able to increase the scale of financial intermediation and reduce system risk following bank restructuring, they typically made less progress in improving the efficiency of financial intermediation. This lack of progress underscores the importance of operational restructuring and of creating appropriate incentives for bank owners, managers, and supervisors and the market to monitor banks and to ensure prudent corporate governance.

## The Economic Issues Series

1. *Growth in East Asia: What We Can and What We Cannot Infer.* Michael Sarel. 1996.
2. *Does the Exchange Rate Regime Matter for Inflation and Growth?* Atish R. Ghosh, Anne-Marie Gulde, Jonathan D. Ostry, and Holger Wolf. 1996.
3. *Confronting Budget Deficits.* 1996.
4. *Fiscal Reforms That Work.* C. John McDermott and Robert F. Wescott. 1996.
5. *Transformations to Open Market Operations: Developing Economies and Emerging Markets.* Stephen H. Axilrod. 1996.
6. *Why Worry About Corruption?* Paolo Mauro. 1997.
7. *Sterilizing Capital Inflows.* Jang-Yung Lee. 1997.
8. *Why Is China Growing So Fast?* Zuliu Hu and Mohsin S. Khan. 1997.
9. *Protecting Bank Deposits.* Gillian G. Garcia. 1997.
10. *Deindustrialization—Its Causes and Implications.* Robert Rowthorn and Ramana Ramaswamy. 1997.
11. *Does Globalization Lower Wages and Export Jobs?* Matthew J. Slaughter and Phillip Swagel. 1997.
12. *Roads to Nowhere: How Corruption in Public Investment Hurts Growth.* Vito Tanzi and Hamid Davoodi. 1998.
13. *Fixed or Flexible? Getting the Exchange Rate Right in the 1990s.* Francesco Caramazza and Jahangir Aziz. 1998.
14. *Lessons from Systemic Bank Restructuring.* Claudia Dziobek and Ceyla Pazarbaşıoğlu. 1998.